# Circle of Wine

*The Only Way to Beat Your Alcohol Addiction*

Greta Kay

Copyright © 2023 by Greta Kay

All rights reserved.

No part of this publication may be reproduced, distributed, or transmitted in any form or by any means, including photocopying, recording, or other electronic or mechanical methods, without the prior written permission of the publisher, except as permitted by U.S. copyright law. For permission requests, contact GretaKayBooks@gmail.com. For privacy reasons, some names, locations, and dates may have been changed.

First edition November 2023

Book Cover illustration by: Gabriele Dabasinskaite

Book Design by: RLS Creativity

Published by: RLS Creativity https://qr.link/7lkNPU

Paperback: 978-1-7390569-2-6

E-book: 978-1-7390569-1-9

# Dedication

*I dedicate this book to my dad, who passed away this year. He was a wonderful, loving man with a great sense of humor and with his own story.*

*Without him and his story, this book would not exist. I know he is guiding me every day of my life and he is inspiring me to do greater things.*

# Contents

| | |
|---|---|
| My Story | vii |
| Introductory Thoughts | xxiii |
| | |
| The Only Way | 1 |
| Step 1: Make a Decision and Stick to It | 3 |
| Step 2: Change Your Mindset | 13 |
| Step 3: Stay on the Right Side | 17 |
| Step 4: Get Healthy | 27 |
| Step 5: Be Aware | 35 |
| Your New Life | 41 |
| If Your Loved One Has an Addiction | 49 |
| | |
| Acknowledgments | 51 |
| About the Author | 53 |

# My Story

Individuals in my family struggled with alcohol addiction my whole life. As far back as I remember, someone was drinking. First—my dad. All my childhood I watched him drink. Every party or friends' gathering ended the same. My dad would get super drunk and then my parents would fight. Sometimes it would get so bad that it would turn into mental and physical abuse. It was so scary. As a child I just couldn't understand why it was happening. I was always scared that my dad would die from drinking too much. I was scared that something would happen to my mom. Sometimes I was even scared for me and my brother. I could not understand why my dad, who was such a great dad when he was sober, could be so cruel when he was drunk. There was so much anger. I begged him to stop so many times. He promised to stop many times. It would always end up the same—him drinking again.

Sometimes when he was drunk, his behavior would change in the matter of seconds. He would go from being nice to so angry, and it did not matter who was in his way—me, my brother, my mom, or anyone else. A couple times, when he got angry, I looked deep into his eyes, crying and trying to understand why he was doing such horrible things. It wasn't him; it was something else in my dad's body, something terrifying, evil. The evil was using his body to do all these horrible things. Ten minutes later it would stop, my dad would look at us and ask, "What happened?"

I could not understand. What do you mean, "What happened?" For the longest time, I just couldn't understand. I was angry as I thought he was lying when he said he couldn't remember. Now I know... Now I understand very well. Now I know he couldn't remember. He would sober up, hear about all the things he did, people he hurt. He would feel so bad and promise us he would never drink again... Only to break that promise a month or two later. And it would happen again, and again, and again. It was a vicious cycle that he couldn't escape.

He would do so well for some time, but after a while, he would always find himself in the same spot again, asking for forgiveness for the things he couldn't even remember he did. He tried to stop. I know he did. He tried everything he knew—he wanted to save his family. I knew he loved us so much, but I could not understand why he couldn't just stop...for us...As a kid I was always in fear, wondering, "When is it going to be the next time? How is it going to end? Will someone get hurt? All I wanted was for it to end, for him to just stop. It went on for years.

Ten years later my dad was still drinking, only now he was not alone. My mom started drinking with him. She said she couldn't take it anymore, so drinking with him made it easier for her, as she didn't care as much. And here I was, as a kid, trying to understand how...how could she ...after all these years of suffering and fighting dad's addiction, now be in the same spot, doing the same thing?

At first it wasn't too bad. She could have a drink or two, or five and it would make her feel better. She wouldn't worry as much. She started not to care that dad drank. She thought it was easier this way. Little did she know she was starting her own vicious, very dangerous cycle that almost killed her so many times and is still fully controlling her life.

The hardest thing for me now is I know how to help her but I'm not able to because she doesn't want to be helped. She doesn't want to stop. She has not decided to stop, and I don't think she ever will. I came to the place where I am OK with it. I tried to save her so many times. I tried by being an example, by talking to her, but in the end—the decision is hers, and only hers. No one can make the decision for someone else or make someone else want to stop.

When my parents drank together, it was a double nightmare for me. As I grew older, I felt it was my responsibility to watch them and save them. Even as an adult I would always be scared to go see them, because I did not know if one of them would be dead or seriously injured. I was scared so many times that you would think I would get used to it, but every time it was a different type of scare. What if this time was the time, I would lose one of them, or maybe both? When my parents decided to get a divorce, it was the best thing that could have happened. For so many years that was my dream. I wanted them to get divorced so they could get better, so I didn't have to be scared for them anymore.

It took 28 years for them to get the divorce and

for my dad to stop. After the divorce my mom got better too, she found her soul mate and seemed happy. She drank occasionally but it did not seem to be a problem anymore.

Dad remarried and stopped drinking for good; he didn't have a drink for 20 years and was healthy and happy. Life blessed him with 20 beautiful years without alcohol. He passed away this year. I'm glad he was able to enjoy life because at one point he decided to stop drinking.

After several years, knowing my parents were better, I moved on with my life. However, before I knew what happened, I started to like drinking myself. At first it was fun. I didn't think much of it. I knew I would never become an alcoholic because of all the things I had gone through as a child. I was sure I would never let my children have the same childhood. At first, I only drank on the weekends and special occasions. Somehow, I found I was always looking forward to those times. I knew I would always end up way more drunk than I should have been, but I still didn't think much of it. I knew I was fine. More years passed, and it seemed that every weekend I now found an occasion or reason to drink. I chose friends that liked drinking. I went places that had alcohol. Slowly I got pulled deeper and deeper into my own vicious cycle. I would party every Friday, Saturday, even drinking on Sunday, though I knew I would feel like crap on Monday. Sometimes I felt so bad that I couldn't go to work. I started to make the worst decisions. People didn't like me anymore, except the ones of course who liked to drink with me or wanted to take advantage of me. Over the years I lost friends who felt embarrassed of me, or just did not want to deal with my addiction anymore. I didn't seem to get into any good relationships with partners, and it only got worse and worse over the years. I had so many short-term relationships or one-night stands, and even though I wanted it to get better, it didn't seem to get any better. I was so unhappy. Years went by. Every year I hoped for a change. At New Year's I would think, "Everything will magically change, and I will have a better year."

I was heavily drinking every day. It was never just a glass of wine. It was a bottle, or two. I could not stop. Every morning, I felt sick and shaky, and I got weaker and weaker. Yet, I could not wait to come home from work to have a glass of wine, which again turned into five or more. I drank myself to sleep every day. I couldn't socialize sober. I couldn't do anything without alcohol. At that point I did not need an occasion to get drunk. Every day itself was a good enough occasion for me. Most of the time, I could not remember anything from the night before. I would wake up in the places I did not know, next to people I did not remember. That would make me feel so sick and ashamed. I would go home and continue drinking just to forget, just to not think about it. At least I tried not to think about it. I tried to trick my mind into thinking nothing happened, but I couldn't. I could drink all I possibly could, but once I sobered up, I knew these thoughts would follow me and never leave me alone. I felt so ashamed. Why did I do that again? I told myself I would never do it again, but yet again, I did.

The more ashamed I felt, the more I drank, and just told myself I did not care what people thought of me. But deep down I did. I really cared. I loved my work, and I was good at it. I had to change jobs often, because sometimes drinking heavily on the weekend turned into a couple days along with a couple days of feeling hungover and sick. Some jobs I would just quit so I could continue drinking for weeks, and after, I would find another one, as it seemed easy for me to do.

After a while I did not need people or friends to drink with me anymore. It was easier to drink alone —no one judged me that way and no one knew how bad my addiction was. I isolated myself from people. I drank until I passed out every night, sometimes all day long, sometimes for days, or weeks straight. I wouldn't eat or drink water or get up. I would wake up, drink alcohol, smoke and pass out again. After several weeks of heavy drinking, I couldn't get up or even drink alcohol anymore. I was dehydrated, weak, and lifeless.

At one point in my life, I had to move back in with my mom, and very soon we realized we could drink together. We knew how bad our addictions were so we would help each other out. We would help each other hide it. It even seemed like fun at first or at least very convenient. No one knew how bad it was behind closed doors, only we did. And that is why we would help each other get alcohol or recover after days of drinking. What we did not know was how deep into the darkness we were sinking.

At that time, I already had a daughter and here I was doing the same things to her as my parents did to me. Even though I knew how scary it was when your mom was drinking and you couldn't rely on her, I still did it. Even though I loved her more than anything in the world, I still drank! And of course, knowing I was doing that to her made me want to drink even more. All she wanted was for me to stop —stop drinking, stop smoking. She wanted me to be a normal mom. I tried; I really did. When I didn't drink I was the best mom, I could be, but I seemed to get pulled back into the same vicious cycle again and again, and I didn't know how and why.

Of course, I promised her and myself that I would stop, but I just couldn't. Something seemed to control my life and I just couldn't get out of that darkness. Evil was in control of my life. That is how strong the evil is. I felt so guilty, every single day. The guiltier I felt, the more I drank, to numb it up, to not feel it, only to sober up and feel double the amount of guilt, every single time. I could not be sober for long periods of time as I could not handle the feeling of guilt. I would sober up enough to go to work and then counted the minutes to get out of work so I could stop at the liquor store on the way home. Money was always tight, and it was hard to find money for rent and food. But somehow, I always found money for alcohol and cigarettes. Now that I think about it, I have no idea how I survived.

Sometimes I watch homeless people now, that are drinking and smoking, and part of me understands why they choose that over food. I am lucky I never ended up on the streets, but I was very close

## My Story

several times. I thank God and my angels that even in the darkness they were protecting me as much as they could. Sometimes I think about places I have been or people I have met, and I wonder how I got out alive.

After several years alcohol started to make me very sick. It took days to recover from drinking heavily for only a day or two. I knew by then I had a bad problem. I tried many different ways to stop. I tried everything people told me—medicine, drinking once a week, once a month, drinking only one glass, not drinking for months. No matter what, I always ended up in the same spot, feeling sick and helpless with enormous amounts of guilt.

When I thought it couldn't get any worse, it did. My mom's soulmate got sick and died, very suddenly. She could not accept that. She wanted to die with him. So, she drank for days, weeks, not eating, not being able to walk, or talk. I had many sleepless nights because she kept asking for just one more drink. So many times, I had to go to the store in the middle of the night to "save" her. Then after a while, the only way she could stop was by going to the hospital for detox. And believe it or not, it was easy. They took her to the hospital, loaded her up with meds for two or three days and she recovered.

And she could drink again. Soon I figured this was an option and I started doing it myself. I would drink all I could for as long as I could and then go to the hospital to feel better fast.

Since I had a daughter, we took turns....One month I drank with no waking up for days, the next month, mom did. We somehow managed to keep the house, pay the bills, and take care of my daughter. But we existed; we did not live. Some days I didn't even want to live anymore, but I was scared to leave my daughter. I asked God to at least let me live until she was eighteen as I knew I wasn't going to last very long.

A lot of times I thought about death, like if I died then, how would people remember me? There would have probably been only a few people that would have showed up at my funeral, and even they would have probably talked about how I did it to myself and how they felt sorry for me. And it would have been true. A lot of people left me because they didn't want to deal with my addiction. The rest I pushed away as I did not want them to get in between me and my addiction. I was fine alone. I didn't need anyone. I had my daughter, I had my mom, saw my dad sometimes, and to me that seemed enough. They knew how bad my addiction was, so, most of the time they tried to help, not judge. One thing I knew was that I did not want to die like this. I wanted to leave something positive behind. I wanted to be remembered as a good person, not someone who drank herself to death.

Just to tell you how bad it was, the ambulance people knew us already. They would come and ask, "Which one is going this time?" One year I was in the hospital for detox fourteen times. Fourteen! When the doctor told me that I was shocked. I didn't even know. One of those times the nurse told me that they had a young woman in hospice next door because of drinking. She was 32 and I was 34 at that time. That opened my eyes to reality. I understood that if I kept drinking like this, I would end up there too. I understood that just because I was still quite young didn't mean it was not going to happen to me.

Another time at the hospital they told me that I had a fatty liver and that I had two choices—stop drinking immediately and it might go back to normal or keep drinking and get liver cirrhosis. Obviously, the second choice meant death to me, and I did not want to die, not just yet. So, the choice was obvious, but the problem was I did not know how to stop.

I existed like this for over a decade. I wanted to stop; I really did... But at the same time, I was scared.

## *My Story*

How could I never drink again? After so many years it seemed impossible. I had a secret desire to somehow find the way to beat this addiction...And deep down I knew I would. And I did...

At age 34, I got pregnant again. It was so scary to me because now I had to stop, not by choice. I didn't drink for 9 months, but of course I could not wait until the day I could drink again. I counted days. I even said I would bring the bottle of wine to the hospital so I could drink right after I delivered the baby. After my son was born, I thought I was cured, because I hadn't had a drink for so long. I figured I could be a social drinker again. I totally believed that!!

It took one month of "social drinking" to end up in the hospital again, for detox. That was my breakthrough. I realized that there was no cure for this. I had tried everything at that point and realized that the only way, the ONLY way is to never have a drink again. The only way to end the vicious cycle was to never start it.

After I came back from hospital that time, I couldn't sleep for a week. Every time I closed my eyes, I kept seeing these visuals like old cartoons that kept replaying the same thing. It sounds crazy but I know I was not crazy. And if you are advanced with your drinking, you probably know the things you must go through when your body is detoxing. I decided to close my eyes and just watch it. I watched it step by step, over and over, and realized it was playing the cycle I was in. The cycle from the moment you take that first drink to the moment your body is too weak to have another one.

This is what I saw. Once a man took a first drink, the little Devil was sitting in that bottle and got into man's body. He was very happy he got in. Then just like a little child he was waiting for food. His food was alcohol. Every time the man drank, he got some food. So, at first, he grew a little as the man would drink sometimes, thinking he could control it. With time the man drank more and more, because of different situations in his life that he thought was contributing to his drinking. He kept choosing the type of alcohol he thought he was craving. All that was happening was the little Devil was demanding food. Day by day the little Devil grew bigger and got stronger, to the point where he was now choosing what the man was going to drink. Until it didn't matter anymore. It was good enough if it was alcohol of any kind. Very soon the man felt weak and sick. He kept drinking now just to try and feel better, just to survive. The Devil though got very strong; he was ready to do some harm. The poor man went around hurting people, doing embarrassing things. The Devil used him as a puppet to walk around, act stupid, and make a fool of himself. People laughed at him, pointed fingers. He kept drinking to the point where he could not even get up anymore. His body was so weak and useless. The Devil then just dropped his body on the side of the road and left him there, lifeless. However, before he left, looking for another victim, he dropped an enormous amount of guilt and shame on the man's body and left. "Until next time" he said....

At first, I couldn't understand why I was seeing it every time I closed my eyes, but then I got it. That was it. This is what happened every time I drank. EVERY TIME. I was like a hamster in the little wheel who keeps running but going nowhere. I was running away from myself. I understood that the ONLY WAY to get out of this cycle was to never get into it. You just never get into that wheel. You stay as far away from that vicious cycle as you can. And the only way to stay out is to never have that first drink!

That night I went downstairs and started writing. I did not know why, but I knew I had to. I knew it was a sign for me. I knew I did not want to forget what I saw. I felt that I finally understood why I kept doing the same thing over again and again. I marked the day. It was November 1, 2015. Somehow, I knew it was the last time I would drink. I knew I would never drink again.

Now that you know my story, you know there is hope. I don't think my story is the worst out there, but I think it is damn bad. I was embarrassed of my story for years until I was able to forgive myself and understand that I could use it to help others. I was able to forgive myself and now I am telling my story with my head held high, with pride and joy that I was able to figure this out. I have nothing to be ashamed of now. I was ashamed then. Now I only have great things to show. I can be an example to others, to show them that there is a light at the end of the tunnel. There is hope. There is a way, and it is EASY—way easier than drinking, I promise you that! When we drink it is like a full-time job. We must get creative at hiding our addiction. And we can get very creative!!! Just like evil that studies our strengths and weaknesses, so he can get creative and use it to make you do some serious harm to yourself and others.

Now I am glad I got to experience it as if I hadn't gone through it myself, I would not be able to help others, to be a success story.

# Introductory Thoughts

Thank you for taking the first step and reading this book. That shows you already have what it takes—a strong desire to stop drinking. It is very hard to admit to yourself that you have a problem with alcohol even though it is most likely already controls your life.

By picking up this book you opened the doors to freedom, freedom from this dark vicious cycle that seems to never end but only get worse each time. This book is a key to being able to beat alcohol addiction and to control it for the rest of your life.

By reading my story you know how strong my addiction was, and understand I know exactly how you feel. You probably feel weak, scared, broken, sad, and out of control. I am not a doctor of any kind; I am just a woman who was in the darkest place in her life and was able to find the way out and change her life forever. It took me years to figure out the way to beat my alcohol addiction and it took me years to write this book. But I cannot wait any longer. I owe this to the world. I know people need it and I must share the only way that I know works. Even if you are reading this book but haven't made the decision to stop drinking yet, at some point you will. Once you do, you will already know how. So, you have nothing to lose. Invest this time into yourself and enjoy the benefits waiting for you. The book is short, and it won't take long to read it. You can try other ways. In fact, you can try to prove this will not work, but after several tries you will know. This is the way; the only way and I am excited to share it with the world.

I wanted to write this book to help people who are struggling with alcohol addiction or have someone close to them who do. I was lucky enough to find the way to stop, forever. Even though I was in such a dark place and struggled for over a decade, I was blessed to find the way out. This same method works for other addictions, including smoking, but I will focus most on alcohol addiction as it was the worst one for me. As I said, I struggled with alcohol

## Introductory Thoughts

addiction for years and every time I wanted to stop, I searched the internet for ways to stop. There was nothing. In fact, there were more articles about why alcohol is good for you and how drinking in moderation can improve your health. I was way past the "drinking in moderation" mark.

I almost drank myself to death several times. It was so bad, that for some people hearing it now makes it very hard to believe. People look at me and think there is no way. But it is true. My addiction was so bad, that I did not believe I could ever stop. I wanted to, I truly did, but I could not find the way. All my weekends and holidays were taken. My time was occupied with drinking which eventually turned into drinking heavily every day, then drinking myself to sleep, and waiting for the next day to drink again. I drank all the time.

I tried so many things I knew, things I heard, things I read. However, I just could not find anything that worked for me. Nothing worked for me. I tried counting my glasses, drinking on the weekends only, occasions only, drinking light or hard liquor, hypnosis, stopping for short and long periods of time. Nothing worked. I would stop for a while, but before I knew it, I was drinking again. It was a vicious, never-ending cycle that kept getting worse

## Introductory Thoughts

with time. When I would stop for some time, I felt I was doing well, until I ended up in the same dark place again—drunk, weak, and hopeless. It was the same dangerous cycle, only a different time, place, or with different people. Eventually I got to the point where I had to choose—to continue like this and die or to find the way to stop.

I was stuck in this never-ending cycle that was controlling my life, taking away my health, my family, my money, my pride, my dignity, my morals, my goals.

I have been sober for over 8 years now and my life is totally different. I went from struggling financially, physically, and mentally to being successful, healthy, and happy. I went from having nothing to having everything I have ever wanted; I went from feeling sick and hopeless to feeling strong and confident. I am looking forward to all these beautiful years ahead of me. I feel obligated to write this book, to save as many people as I can, and even if it only saves one person, it will be worth it.

Read this book even if you are not ready to stop yet. It is not going to hurt. At the end of the day, it is always your decision. No one can make that decision for you. Read it again as you feel the need. Read it if you are on the right track and times get tough. Read

## Introductory Thoughts

it if you fail and need to gain your strength back. You can fail, but you never give up. Read this book even if you feel great—read it to be proud of yourself, to remind yourself that you are a winner and celebrate!

I will tell you the steps and walk you through each of them. I will tell you the only way to stop this dangerous cycle. I think every addiction is different, but also the same. The struggle is real and unless you are an alcoholic yourself, it is almost impossible to understand how hard it is to stop drinking.

When you drink, you live two different lives. One is full of secrets, pain, guilt, denial, lies, shame, and that never-ending vicious cycle that just drags you deeper into the darkness. The other one where you must act like a regular person, go to work, talk to people, try to act normal, but really all you can think of is going back home so you can have a drink. You keep trying to juggle between those two and trying to survive, but the hope to escape the darkness keeps fading away. It is so dark that you can barely see the light. You are trying to stay strong, but some days you feel it is not even worth it. You feel like you will never be able to get out of this vicious cycle. But let me tell you—you will! Read this book and you will see the light at the end of the tunnel. You will be stronger than ever and so damn proud of yourself!

## Introductory Thoughts

It took me years of procrastination to start writing this book, which originally, I thought would only be an article. Now I know I cannot wait any longer and I cannot wait to get it out to the world. I know the demand is there and people are looking to find the way to stop. I want to help people around the world beat their addiction, help them change their lives forever, help them see how beautiful life can truly be. It took me years to find the only way to stop, and if you are reading this book, you are on the way to freedom—freedom from addiction that is keeping you hostage in your own life.

You are on the way to a life full of happiness, love, strength, fulfillment, joy, light, health, and respect.

Some people are ashamed of their story. Some people are surprised how brave I am to tell mine. I used to be ashamed, but I have nothing to be ashamed of now. Now I can only be proud of myself. I am happy I have a story to tell that can change the lives of others.

# The Only Way

Are you ready to choose YOU?! If you are, then read and follow these steps with a 100% commitment and never look back. You cannot skip or alternate any of the steps. There are only 5 of them and this is the ONLY WAY!

1. Make a decision and stick to it.
2. Change your mindset.
3. Always choose the right side.
4. Get healthy.
5. Be aware.

You've got this!

# Step 1: Make a Decision and Stick to It

Deciding to stop drinking is one of the most important and one of the hardest decisions you will make in your life. The first step is to realize you have a problem with alcohol and to decide to stop.

Deep down inside you will know when you are ready. And, unless YOU are ready, there is nothing and no one that can make that decision for you. Only you know when it is time. And even if you are not ready now, at some point you will be and after reading this book you will know how to. Deep down I know you are ready. It is probably your dream to stop, to not have to feel the pain, weakness, guilt, and misery every single day. Good news! There is a way, and it is easier than you think. Everyone can do it.

I know it is scary and challenging. It took me years to make the decision, but once I figured this whole thing out, I knew it was the best decision I could have ever made, and I never looked back. Even though you probably don't feel like it now, you CAN be in control. You CAN beat this addiction. And even though evil is very strong, you are way stronger. Good always wins, no matter what. Once you beat this addiction, you will know what I mean. I cannot wait for you to experience all the good things this life can bring. I cannot wait for you to be proud of yourself and show everyone else how strong you really are.

A lot of you have secret lives. You struggle with alcohol by yourselves all alone in the darkness, scared and weak. You seem to have a normal life outside the house, but all you want to do is go home and have a drink. That one drink usually turns into two or three, or... you drink till you fall asleep, and you even think it helps you fall asleep. Then you realize it wakes you up early in the morning so you can feel the pain. Every day you are guessing how bad your next morning is going to be. Your health is getting worse and worse every day. You seem to not want to socialize as much. You feel guilty. In the

## Step 1: Make a Decision and Stick to It

morning you feel so bad, you tell yourself you will never drink again, but very soon you do, and you do it again, and again.

This is a cycle that never ends. You might stop for a day or two, or a month, but before you know what happened, you are back to that same vicious cycle which seems to be getting worse each time. How long you will last depends on how strong the health is you were born with. Some die very young, not being able to have a chance to enjoy life or to even know what a good life is. Some drive drunk, accidentally kill someone and spend their life in jail. You know what is going to happen if you continue like this, but somehow choose not to think about it. You choose to ignore it, almost like you bury your head in the sand, thinking no one can see you, but you know everyone can. YOU know what is going on.

Some of you think somehow it is not going to happen to you, but deep down you know you will die soon if you don't make the right choice. I know every alcoholic wants to stop even if they say they don't. How many times did you tell yourself or others you were not drinking again? Yet before you knew it you did, and you were back at it full force... You are not the only one. There are thousands of us.

And until you stop you are not in control, evil is, and the more addictions you have the stronger it is.

For example, if you smoke, that's double the power. Just think how many times you quit smoking. You were so proud of yourself. You didn't smoke for a week, a month. You have a drink or two and you don't even remember how you end up with the pack of cigarettes and here you are, smoking again. It might start with one cigarette a day, or a week. You may think you are now in control, and you can smoke whenever you want to, but before you know you buy a pack and you are smoking as much as you did before, or more, because now you feel guilty and disappointed in yourself. Good thing my method works for all addictions, smoking too. And once you beat your addictions, you will be in control! Full control. I don't suggest quitting both at the same time, but I will explain more later in the book.

Some people tend to think and tell others that a drink or two a day is good for your health, because they read an article about it, or their friends told them about it. I will tell you the truth – there is absolutely NOTHING in alcohol that is good for the human body! All these articles are probably paid for by the companies that produce and sell alcohol to make you think it is good for you, to make your addiction stronger. The more addicted you are, the more money they make. I have even heard that lately they have been adding more spirit, nicotine, and chemicals that make your addiction worse and it is that much harder to quit. They do that because more and more people are trying to quit. If you think about it, especially red wine (that people think is the healthiest) is the worst. It is a certain concentration of spirit diluted with water and a lot of red color. Yes, that is exactly why your lips stay red after you drink it and it is hard to wash out of clothes. There might be some real red wine out there made from grapes, but that one is way too expensive for an average person to buy. At some point I switched to red wine too, as I thought it was at least a healthier option. It was way worse for me. It made me way sicker every time I drank it.

I think all of us that have any type of addiction always carry that little Devil inside of us. The one that tells us to drink, smoke, or use drugs.

I already talked about how important the initial decision is, but as important as it is to make the decision the first time, it is even more important to stick to it. That means you keep making the right decision every single day. So now that you know the only way to grow the little Devil inside of you (your addiction) bigger is to feed it with alcohol, what decision are you going to make every time you THINK you want a drink? If you know it is not even you craving alcohol, but it's that Devil demanding food, what choice are you going to make? Are you going to choose evil and let him grow bigger to be able to control your life, or are you going to choose YOU and grow stronger and stay in control? For me the choice is simple every single time. I choose to keep him so small that his voice is funny and irrelevant to me.

Every time you think you want a drink, stop, and think:

- Do you want to end up at the same place you were before?
- Do you want to feel like crap again?

Most of the time that will be enough to make a right decision, if not here is more:

- Is it worth losing everything you have?
- Is it worth dying?
- Is it worth feeling like you are in hell while you are still alive?

*Step 1: Make a Decision and Stick to It*

NO, NO, and NO.

Absolutely not!

You deserve light.

You deserve happiness.

You deserve to live and enjoy living.

So, keep making that choice every day. Be grateful for every day you have and make the best out of it. Be proud of yourself and watch how everything is changing around you.

The choice is yours:

Do you choose life or death?

Do you choose yourself?

I choose health and a clear mind. I choose ME! That is the decision and choice I make every single day and there is nothing on this earth that can change it.

NOTE: *If you are reading this book because of your loved one fighting an alcohol addiction, please know that you cannot make the decision for them or force them to make it. If they are not ready, this will not work. So, unless they are ready, there is absolutely nothing you can do, besides staying by their side, waiting until they are ready. You have your own decisions to make—how long are you willing to wait? Are you willing to stay after they make that decision? It seems like an easy decision now, but trust me, you might change your mind later. I will explain more later in the book.*

Know that they might never make that decision or make it when it is too late. So, please put yourself first. Believe it or not, you have absolutely nothing to do with their problem. Sometimes they don't either. It could be so many different factors, like family history, genetics, karma, lifestyle, previous heartbreaks, and stress. Some of them can be controlled, like stress, lifestyle and people close to us. Some cannot, like genetics, karma from previous lives, family history.

Whatever the reason, one day they will be ready to stop, hopefully not too late. Once they decide to stop, you will have a very hard and long journey ahead of you if you decide to stay with them and help them through it. Please know you don't have to. It is their problem, and they must deal with it. As harsh as it sounds, it is their life, and you have yours to take care of. I know it is hard for you to understand now. Why wouldn't you stick with them? Probably all you ever wanted is for them to stop. Well, it is extremely hard for them in the beginning, and it is even harder for you, especially because you don't know what addiction really is. The person you

*Step 1: Make a Decision and Stick to It*

knew will change. They will be a different person for a while, and you might not even like that person. Now, whatever the situation, the decision must be made by the person who is addicted to alcohol, not you, or anything else in this book will not matter.

## Step 2: Change Your Mindset

This step is as important as making the initial decision. It is not worth deciding, going through detox, and then not being able to enjoy the benefits because your life is miserable. Some people feel like a victim after they stop drinking. They feel that something was taken away from them and now everyone is supposed to feel sorry for them because they can`t drink. You can tell they want to drink, but they know they can`t so they hate other people who can. They feel sad and depressed and want everyone else to stop drinking too, because it bothers them. They say, "Oh I can`t drink ever again. Everyone else can but me; I am such a victim".

**You are not a VICTIM; you are a WINNER!**

**Always remember this and never let yourself think otherwise.**

**So, teach yourself to feel and act like a winner**.

If you think you CAN'T drink you are going to want to, all the time, and that is extremely hard. That is torturing yourself for no reason. That is punishing yourself for doing the right thing. Just like kids, if they can't have something, they want it even more. What helped me over the years was knowing and telling myself that I can drink just like everyone else. I can go to the store right now, buy alcohol and drink it all at once.

Nothing is stopping me, but I CHOOSE not to, and that is a big difference.

- I CHOOSE the lifestyle I have now over the one I had before.
- I CHOOSE to be healthy over sick all the time.
- I CHOOSE to be the best mom I can be over a shitty one.
- I CHOOSE happiness over misery.

## Step 2: Change Your Mindset

- I CHOOSE life over death.
- I CHOOSE light over darkness.
- I always CHOOSE ME.
- I am more important than alcohol and I will not change my mind!

So, for me it is not even a fight anymore. I know it is my choice so why would I feel sad about it? You should feel happy and proud. That is the point!

It doesn't bother me at all when other people drink; that's their choice. I make my own choices. I think they look and act funny and stupid when they drink too much. I feel sad for the ones I know have a problem with alcohol but are too embarrassed to ask for help or admit it. I want to jump in and save them all, but I just can't, because they are not ready. Hopefully this book will reach them one day.

Nowadays it is way easier not to drink than it was before. A lot of people don't drink anymore. Fewer people ask why people don't drink. In the beginning it was hard for me as everyone would look at me strange when I said I didn't drink. They would ask questions, make fun, say I should drink with them, say I could get drunk with them just one time. To them it was funny; to me it was painful. It was hard enough to say no, and now on top of that I had to explain myself. So, if you have people next to you that drink a lot and don't understand and support your decision, kindly eliminate them from your life, at least for now, until you get stronger. With time you will understand that most people who don't support you are not good friends. Most likely the ones that don't support you are struggling with their own demons, and it has nothing to do with you. And if they keep asking, tell them you choose life and walk away. They are not important; YOU are.

# Step 3: Stay on the Right Side

As we all know there are two opposite sides in this world—good and bad. One is controlled by God and the other by evil. Every one of us chooses which side we are on. Every time we make any kind of decision, say any kind of words it is usually good or bad. Depending on the majority of your choices and your lifestyle you choose one of the sides.

The good side is kindness, joy, beauty, love, happiness, wealth, health, harmony, peace, and forgiveness.

The bad one is darkness, sadness, guilt, hate, pain, sickness, failure, loneliness, and poverty.

So, which one do you want to stay on?

If the bad side sounds good to you right now, you

don't have to do anything. You are on the right track, and you have nothing to change. You know exactly where you are going and how you will end up.

If you are on the good side, you are probably reading this book trying to help someone else.

If you are on the bad side and are trying to get over to the good side, you are on the right track and you will soon know how.

I think all of us have a little of the bad inside of us. We all do things we regret or hurt people we didn't mean to hurt. Sometimes we even think, "How could we do such a thing?" Well, you already know who helps you there. Evil is a very powerful thing and alcohol is one of the strongest tools it uses to control people and do some serious harm. So usually where is alcohol, there is evil. That's why people who drink a lot have all these bad things happening to them or around them. Even if they don't drink often, when they do, they will do some stupid stuff they regret. They hurt someone's feelings, get in a fight, cheat, lose money, make bad decisions, are involved in bad deals, and meet bad people.

Some people seem to be able to control their drinking. Or at least they think they do. I say these people have a lazy Devil next to them that just

## Step 3: Stay on the Right Side

doesn't feel like working hard, or at least not yet—not until something happens in that person's life and all the sudden they turn into an alcoholic. There is a part of the Devil in each of us that have an addiction; it just depends how big it is and how active it wants to be.

If you choose alcohol and evil, you will stay on the dark side, and things will go wrong in your life. Most likely you will have days when everything seems good and starts to get better, and all the sudden it will all fall apart again. And yet again, another good reason to drink. Some people drink to get rid of stress or to numb sorrows and problems. They soon find out that sorrows and problems are still going to be there after they sober up, and now they are not as strong and focused to try and solve those issues.

If you choose alcohol you will stay in the lowest frequency levels, which can only attract low frequency things. You will attract hate, poverty, cruelty, sickness, struggle, bad relationships, and it will stay that way, unless you make a choice to move to the other side.

So, the decision is yours to make. It must be a strong decision, not a maybe, not I will try. It must be a 100%. God knows when you are ready, he is waiting. And once you make that decision, everything will start changing.

All good things will start happening, everything will start falling into place, and you will start building the life you always wanted. Now you are on God's side and he will always be there to help you. Even though evil is strong, God is ALWAYS stronger, always will be. Good always wins. The hardest part is deciding and continuing to make the choices to stay on the right side every day of your life. God will help you along the way.

Once you make a right choice, all the right people will start appearing at the right place, at the right time. Your health will start improving. Your mindset is going to change. You will get stronger every day. You will start receiving all these gifts from the universe. Your health, financial situation, friends, and surroundings will improve and if you are smart enough to notice it and be grateful for it, there are no limits to your success. Do yourself a favor and look around. Find all the positive changes, notice all the positive feelings, notice the signs from God and enjoy every single moment. Don't get stuck in a victim position feeling miserable, it is not worth it! You deserve better!

## Step 3: Stay on the Right Side

So, what do you have to do to get to the good side?

Follow the five steps!

It is easier than you think, and everyone can do it. At first it might seem hard, but once you start experiencing the rewards and freedom, it will be easier every day.

And you know what can get you back to the dark side very quickly?

ONE DRINK.

Yes, you can decide to get better and stay on the good side, but you can also decide to have one little drink and end up back on the dark side as fast as you finish that one drink. If you choose to have one drink, it is only a matter of time before you end up on the dark side, struggling all alone in the darkness again. You will probably end up in a worse place than you were before. There are no exceptions! You will have to start over again.

I always say there are no shortcuts in this life. Don`t try to outsmart the system and think that you can be on both sides and still get the rewards. If you think you can secretly have a drink or two and no one will know, you are wrong.

STOP now! There is no such thing. God knows; YOU know! You CANNOT cheat yourself. If you try to be a smartass and beat the system, the system will beat you and you will pay the price. So, if you are still having those thoughts your decision is not final. Go back to step one and rethink your decision.

If you still feel strongly about your decision read this again. I mentioned this in the beginning, but I want to explain it again, as it is very important to understand how this vicious cycle works and how to avoid getting into it.

## The dangerous cycle

Every time you decide to have that first drink again, you let the little Devil enter your body. Imagine him sitting in your belly, very happy he was able to get in. He is like a baby waiting for his food, which is alcohol or drugs. In the beginning it is so small that you get to choose what you want to drink and how often. Every time you drink again, he gets stronger and stronger, and before you know what happened, he dictates what you are going to drink today and how often. That is when you start feeling that strong urge to drink, always. It is him, demanding food. Once he gets strong, he starts to control your life, and your decisions, making you do the horrible things you would never do sober, making the worst deci-

## Step 3: Stay on the Right Side

sions you would never make sober, going to all the places to get alcohol which seems to get worse and worse. Usually, alcohol makes you attack the people you love the most, people who are closest to you, people who keep giving you another chance. He wants you to get rid of them because most likely they are in the way, trying to stop you from drinking. It wants you to hurt them, so they leave, so you can freely drink more and more and do more harm. If you watch drunk people, you can see, they are like puppets controlled by the Devil. They dance funny, they act like clowns, they make a fool of themselves. Fights start when people are drunk. Everywhere where is alcohol, there is evil. After a while you start drinking every day, and if you are weaker like I was, it turns into heavy nonstop drinking quickly. Then you drink for weeks without water or food, not remembering two weeks out of your life at all. After a couple weeks of drinking your body is just too weak to drink anymore and do more harm so he leaves your body lifeless and throws an enormous amount of guilt on top of it, just to make sure you feel the pain when you sober up.

He leaves until next time... Until you start feeling better and usually about a month later you feel like you want to have a drink again, just one.

And once you decide to pick up that drink, it all starts all over again. It's a cycle. It is just a matter of time before you will end up in the same spot again, feeling weak and ashamed, asking for forgiveness, asking for another chance...

I hope you are lucky like I was. I hope you stop on time. I hope you get to see how beautiful the other side is, the side of light, the side of God. If you are reading this book, you still have a chance. Once you decide and get on the good side, you will understand what I was talking about. You will understand why I wanted you to see it.

Choose the people who are close to you wisely. You will see right away who is on your side and will support you on your new journey and who is on the other side, trying to get you back there. Most likely these people are there themselves and are not ready to cross over. How many times do you see your friends nodding their head with a smile when you say you are trying to stop, because they hope you don't? And why? Because they probably tried to quit a couple of times and failed, and you failing makes them feel better about themselves. It helps them think that they are not the only ones who can't stop.

Know that you don't need those people in your life. Even if it's family. You can't choose your family, but you can choose if you want them in your life. If you stick around the people who are trying to drag you back into the dark side, it will be easy for you to fail. You must be careful and always choose YOU. Choose life! If they are trying to get you back into the dark side, they are not your friends, they are friends with evil. Most likely after you stay sober for a while you won't even have anything in common. You will have nothing to talk to them about. So, at end of the day what is the point of keeping those people close to you and risking your sobriety? If they are still drinking, the Devil is always right next to them, and if you stay close you will be affected. I don't want anything to do with the Devil anymore so I stay as far away as possible.

I don't judge other people; They have their choices and I always have mine. If they choose to stay on the dark side, I choose not to have them in my life. It's that simple. I choose me! In the future if they decide to get out of the vicious cycle, I can tell them how. I would love to help.

# Step 4: Get Healthy

As we know, alcoholism is a disease, and I like to compare it to cancer. You feel horrible while you are sick, and you know it is going to kill you. You just don't know how fast and how painful your death will be. It spreads around too and drags other people into the vicious cycle. You would do anything to cure it, but you don't know how.

What if we told people who have cancer there was one thing they had to stop drinking or eating and the cancer would go away? Do you think they would do it? They would, without a doubt.

Alcoholism is a very serious disease, but you are lucky because there is a cure for it. All you must do is never drink alcohol again! That is how simple it is.

You don't even HAVE to do anything; you just must NOT drink. That is the same for drugs and cigarettes.

Once you decide and change your mindset, it is way easier than you think. At first you might want a nonalcoholic drink to substitute for it, which is ok. There is nothing wrong with that. Some people say you shouldn't do it because it is very easy to go from nonalcoholic to alcoholic. It was never a problem for me. I decided alcohol is not an option for me, so in the beginning while I thought I was still craving that taste, I was drinking nonalcoholic drinks, and I was perfectly fine. After several years you don't even want it anymore, because you realize the taste is not that great and there are a bunch of chemicals used to remove alcohol, so there is no reason for drinking that. But anytime you feel like you want a glass of something there are plenty of nonalcoholic options out there these days. You will feel so great sober that you will want to keep feeling great.

With time you will want to feel even healthier and stronger so you will slowly change your diet and start exercising. It almost becomes another addiction, an addiction to be healthy. And I will choose that addiction any day of my life over any other.

Now let me tell you a secret.

## Step 4: Get Healthy

**It only takes 17 days** for your body to fully remove any alcohol. What this means is that any trace of alcohol is gone in 17 days so there is ABSOLUTELY no way you could crave it after that.

So, all you must do is decide—choose to get on the right side and count the days.... it's only 17!

Prepare yourself for that time. You may feel angry, lonely, and sad. You might need to isolate yourself from others, or get people close to you to stay closer. You may want to eat more foods or drink more fluids. You might experience physical withdrawals. Whatever it takes, YOU'VE GOT THIS!

If you have a right mindset, it will be easier!

If at any time after 17 days you feel that you crave alcohol, it is a FALSE craving. You must recognize it and be ready. Here is what you do. You simply drink water or eat something; it will go away! That simple!

Your body is not able to crave POISON and alcohol is pure poison to our bodies. If you know that it is a false craving trying to confuse you, you will be ok. Just like you can't imagine yourself craving gasoline, there is just no way your body would crave alcohol. You know how bad it is for you, so you know it is not true. You are thirsty or hungry and that is it.

In the beginning you might need more water as

your body is trying to get rid of the toxins and more food because you must offset the calories you would consume with alcohol. Most likely you will lose some weight, which is a great win. When you recognize these false cravings, eat or drink something that you like. Reward yourself for recognizing it and making the right decision. It doesn't mean you get to eat all junk food and cakes all day but reward yourself in moderation. In the beginning, whatever it takes! But you still want to feel strong and healthy, not miserable eating all kinds of crap. With time, as I said, you will probably want to feel healthy and strong so you will make better choices.

I must warn you that it is not going to always be easy. You will struggle in the beginning! Your mind and body are used to being numb to a lot of things, to not have to face the reality sometimes. It will be tough mentally and physically. It will be tough having to experience every feeling and situation without being able to quickly numb it with alcohol. You will have to face reality.

You might see some change in your health as your body is detoxing and healing. Your body will be in shock. You will start feeling all the things you haven't felt before, like pain, stomach, or heart problems, you might experience change in voice, taste.

## Step 4: Get Healthy

These are problems that were there before. They were just numbed with alcohol and/or cigarettes, so you didn't feel it.

That is how people who drink a lot feel fine for the longest time, but then suddenly, they die or get seriously ill. Hopefully you still caught it in time and will be able to fix your health. That depends on a lot of factors. Please don't expect to drink for thirty years, then quit and feel 100% healthy. You will have some consequences, but hopefully yours are not too bad. When I quit smoking, I gained a lot of weight and at first I was upset, but now I am thankful that was the only thing so far that I must deal with for smoking over 25 years. I will take it and I will deal with it! I must do more things that make me stronger, like exercise and eat healthy food. I was lucky and hope you are too. So, the sooner you get out of this crazy cycle, the more chance you have. And either way you will have more years left than you would have if you continued drinking.

I had five different things that went wrong with me. I was wondering why. I was angry, like I never had problems with these organs before. Why now, when I am trying to do the right thing? Well, I did have problems; I just didn't feel it. These problems are all temporary; it all goes away. Remember you are on the other side now. God is always with you. Everything will heal, you will be stronger than ever, and then you will thank God you stopped on time. You earned yourself at least some extra years of life that will be beautiful, joyful, healthy, and enjoyable. You've got this! You are not alone.

Don't be afraid to tell your story. Talk to others. There are way more people struggling with addictions than you can imagine. Choose what works for you. Everyone is different. AA never worked for me, but it works for other people. You must try different things and see what works best. Try to improve your spiritual health as it will help you stay stronger and understand what life is about. If you are into spiritual stuff already you probably know we don't have just one life, and they say if you don't get rid of your addiction in this life, you must deal with it again in the next one. So, I would rather get rid of it in this one, so I don't have to deal with it again. It is just way too hard. It gets in the way of everything you are trying to do. Maybe try some challenges. That will keep your mind busy, and you will feel great after. The better you feel about your body, the easier it is going to be to control your mind. Do anything that makes you feel like a winner. Every small win counts. You can count days that you haven't had

## Step 4: Get Healthy

alcohol, but honestly, I don't. Once you stop counting, you know you are done. It doesn't matter anymore, you just know you are not drinking again, so what is the difference? I must count years each time someone asks me. Honestly, I have no idea how long it has been since I quit smoking—maybe four years, maybe more. I wrote the day when I stopped drinking, but not the last time I smoked. That is not important to me; my future is!

## Step 5: Be Aware

Take control of your addiction, or addiction will take control of you!

Once you follow all the steps of deciding, changing your mindset, choosing the good side, getting healthy, I need you to know that you ALWAYS must be aware. You cannot completely cure the addiction. You can only keep it under control. Remember there is a very fine line between the two sides, which is one drink.

Once you get it all under control and feel strong, you still must be very careful at all times. If you had addictions, that little Devil will always be sitting on your shoulder, ALWAYS. If you had a couple of addictions, there will be a couple of them. They will always be watching, waiting for you to have a weak moment. They will get very creative to lure you into drinking or smoking again. Every time you hear their voices telling you to just have that one drink, you always must go back to step one, DECISION, and make the choice:

- Do you want the life you have now, or the life you had before?
- Do you want to feel the way you felt before, or the way you feel now?
- Do you want to keep the things you have now, or lose everything?
- Do you want to keep the relationships you have now, or go back to being lonely?

You always have a choice!
The choice is yours!
For me the decision is very easy every time and it gets easier and easier with time. And always remember what happens when you choose to have that one drink, smoke that one cigarette? It all starts over again. You get yourself back in the cycle you can't get out of. THERE ARE NO EXCEPTIONS. It is just a matter of time until you end up at the bottom again, sick, weak, worthless, with an enor-

## Step 5: Be Aware

mous amount of guilt, hating yourself for giving up, feeling like a total looser...And that is why I call it The Vicious Circle of Wine. Unless you never start the cycle, you will always be stuck in it, running away from your own self, just like that little hamster. This is the ONLY WAY... there are no other ways, trust me. I tried them all—not one time, not ten, but tens of times. I did it again and again and again, hoping the next time would be different. It is always the same, it never changes, it's just that you get weaker, so it makes you feel worse and worse each time.

The only way, and I can promise you, the ONLY WAY is to never have that first drink again. The only way to kill the Devil is to make him starve each day, that way he remains very small and becomes weaker every day, and you...you become stronger, and you take over the control!

If you have any type of addiction, you will always have an addictive personality, so you must be careful as you will most likely pick up another addiction soon. So, choose wisely. Make sure you choose a good addiction, not another bad one. There are a lot of good addictions out there for you to choose from. You have a healthy lifestyle, gym, work, or a hobby. Just stay away from things like gambling or other bad addictions, like smoking, drugs, sex etc. It is very important you watch yourself closely and be ready. If you feel you are leaning towards one of the bad addictions, go back to step one, DECISION, and make a choice. Do you really want to get another addiction on your shoulders and start the process all over again? The answer is no. Get yourself an addiction that will make you healthy, bring you money or happiness.

This method works for any addiction, but you would have to start over again. One addiction you must know is not curable is gambling, so stay far away from that one.

If you have a couple addictions like drinking and smoking, I do not suggest quitting both at the same time, It's just too much mentally and physically. You might simply go crazy. You sometimes see people who were drinking and smoking and after they stopped, they are just strange. I am sure they are still way happier than before, but if you can avoid that, why not. One addiction at a time. It's hard enough to quit one; two at the same time is just too much. I tried quitting smoking several times, but since I was still drinking, the next time I got drunk, I wouldn't even remember how I got a pack of cigarettes, and I woke up the next morning smelling like smoke. I was

## Step 5: Be Aware

so upset with myself. And of course, that was another good reason for a drink and another cigarette.

The only way that worked for me was quitting drinking first. That way I was sober all the time, and I knew I could at least smoke. I honestly did not think I would ever quit smoking. It was just too hard for me; I tried so many times. But several years after quitting drinking, I wanted to quit smoking too. Once you feel healthier, you just want to be healthier and healthier. I always said I would never exercise or take cold showers. Now I find myself wanting to do things I never wanted to do. Once you get stronger you feel so great that you trust yourself to try new things and get stronger every day.

Guilt is another thing we must deal with daily. The amount of guilt I felt every day because of smoking was just too much for me. I would count cigarettes and smoke only every so many hours, but after I did, I would suddenly feel so guilty that I wanted to smoke again. Like I could not imagine myself in a hospital bed dying of the disease caused by smoking and telling my kids, "Yeah sorry guys, I did it to myself." That was my choice. I just couldn't do it to myself, couldn't do it to them.

I made a mistake by quitting smoking and

starting vaping. I feel that's another very strong chemical that is so powerful and so bad for you, but because its odorless you don't think it is as bad. It is so new that no one really knows much about it yet. What I can tell you from my personal experience is that it was harder to quit that than anything else. When you vape you don't get the same feeling as you did after smoking a cigarette, so you keep vaping all the time, just to try and get the same feeling. When I quit vaping, the first month was brutal. I felt like the nicotine was being sucked out of my brain. I felt like I was going crazy, I couldn't even focus when driving or working. After that I gained a lot of weight, but as I always say if that's the only thing that I will have to deal with for smoking so many years (twenty-five) I will take it! Now I exercise more, eat healthier and the extra weight is slowly going away.

## Your New Life

re you ready to follow the steps, get out of that vicious cycle and enjoy your life? Here are the steps again:

1. Make a decision.
2. Change your mindset.
3. Always choose the right side
4. Get healthy.
5. Be aware.

And most important remember to always choose YOU!

Enjoy every minute of your new life and see how beautiful it can truly be. Start planning your weekends and holidays since now they are available for you; they are no longer taken... Forgive yourself as you cannot change the past and move on. Reward yourself, take the money you would have spent on your addiction, save it, and travel or buy something you always wanted. Find your true purpose in life. That is what life is about. Finding your purpose, helping people, and enjoying everything along the way!

In the beginning things will change and you will feel out of place. There will be things that you will not be able to do for a while, but it's temporary. You might not be able to socialize as much as you did before. For me it was dancing. I love to dance, but I couldn't dance for about four years after I stopped drinking. I just couldn't. I felt shy; it didn't feel right. My body wouldn't move the same. Now I can dance more than I used to. I love dancing and I don't have to have a drink to enjoy it. After a while you will start watching people who drink and see how their bodies are controlled by evil. The Devil uses them like puppets to have fun. All the fights, anger and horrible things happen under the influence. People drive and kill someone, and after they realize what they did, they must live with it their whole lives. So, if such horrible things haven't happened to you yet, you are lucky, you got out on time. Be thankful for that and be proud of yourself. You decided at the right time.

## There May Be Accidents

There may be accidents. Even though I am very careful every time I order a drink, or someone brings me one, there were two times during my journey when I accidentally took a sip of alcohol. Please know, there is a huge difference between accidentally taking a sip and choosing to have one drink thinking nothing will happen. Because remember you cannot fool yourself and since you are sober now, you always know what you are doing.

One time I asked for a virgin margarita at the restaurant and the lady didn't understand English too well. She brought a drink; I smelled it, seemed fine. But once I took a sip, I knew something was wrong; it tasted different. I asked other people to taste the drink and they said it was fine. But I knew it was not. When the waitress came back, we asked her if the drink had alcohol in it, and sure enough she said yes. She said sorry and quickly left to get a new drink like it was not a big deal. I was in shock. My whole life flashed in front of my eyes. And even though it was one sip, I knew one drink could get me right back where I was, into the dark side. I got so scared. I was crying so hard; I did not know what to do. I had a panic attack. Everyone was looking at me not understanding what the big deal was. I just kept crying and I left. I got in the car and stopped myself. I told myself I was strong, and I would be ok. I told myself there was no way I was going back. There was no way I was going to lose everything I have. I got myself together and I was fine. I knew what to do. I knew I was strong enough. I knew I would be ok. I made myself forget about that incident quickly. I knew it was an accident.

About a year later I went to a new church. As usual they had a communion ceremony. I did not know how they did things, so I even asked the people I knew, to make sure it wasn't wine they were giving you during communion. Nobody knew and said probably no. I even went to the priest and as he was giving me bread for the body of Christ I asked if there was alcohol in the cups. He looked at me but didn't say anything. He did not understand what I was asking. SO, I assumed it was safe. I took the bread, and I drank the juice symbolizing the blood of Christ and sure enough it was wine, not the juice like they had at my old church. On the way back to my seat I was terrified. I was so scared. I told myself,

"I just screwed up." I couldn't think of anything else. I just got on my knees and started praying. I asked God to help me. God knew I did not do it on purpose. This was a church, and I truly did not know. Again, I got myself together. I told myself I was strong enough and I would be ok. I was ok, but for the next week sure enough I had the little voices telling me "See nothing happened, you are fine, so maybe you can have a little sip of the wine every Sunday. It is the blood of Christ, nothing will happen." I quickly recognized it, and it just reassured me how strong the evil is, how creative it can be. They were trying to get me back into the cycle! That is why you must always be aware and, in all places, even church. You must know the difference between God's voice and the voice of the Devil, trying yet once again. Maybe, maybe this time you will have that one drink and get back in the vicious cycle. That is how some people who were sober for ten, twenty years go back to drinking just the way they were drinking before—after one drink. And they don't know how. This is exactly how. One accident. One voice you didn't recognize. One mistake. One drink can get you right back quickly.

When my dad died earlier this year, that same second I found out about it I had the strongest urge to smoke. I haven't smoked for years, and I did not want anything to do with it anymore. I was so upset. In such a moment of sadness, they still tried. How rude... They haven't tried since. I think they are scared to 😊 but even if they do, they are not going to succeed—not today, not tomorrow, not ever! I choose life, and I will keep choosing life, I will keep choosing ME...

## Dealing with Guilt

Guilt is something that will follow you for years after you stop. So, get rid of it as quickly as possible. It is not worth it. Somehow when you are drinking or right after you don't remember many things. You are scared to think about all the things you have done. I had it all blocked for years. You are just too embarrassed to remember; you cannot face the truth. After years you will start remembering all the things you did or said to hurt other people, all the things you did to make a fool of yourself, the things you were embarrassed of. Just know, your brain only allows you to remember things if it knows it safe. It means you are strong enough to process it and forgive yourself. Every time I remember some embarrassing moments, I think "What was I thinking!" Do yourself a huge favor and forgive yourself. The sooner you do it, the better. It was not you who did all these horrible things, it was evil using your body to do harm. You cannot change anything in the past, but you can change the future. You can change today, so why not enjoy it? Why not be proud of yourself for not making the same mistakes anymore? People you hurt will forgive you and if not, it is OK if you forgive yourself. That is what is most important.

You will see how people start looking up to you. Some people will even think you had it easy. Some will envy your life. That's why I always say, "You cannot judge people, because you do not know where they are coming from, what life they had before, what they had to do to get where they are right now."

There were times in my life when I barely had money for food for my kids, there were times I lived in the car. When I tell that to people now, they don't believe me. They think I am just saying it to get attention. Now I own my own company, I am the best mom I can be, I am wealthy enough not to worry about money, and when I meet people from my past, I know how well I am doing by the look in their eyes, by how surprised they are. They probably thought I was dead or homeless by now. Sometimes I meet people that I used to drink with, and they are not looking too good. That just shows me where I would have been if I didn't make a choice. And that keeps me going, keeps me wanting to help other people, help them change their lives, get out of darkness, and see the other side.

I thank my past, my strength, all the experiences, all the people who judged me, who pushed me away, who laughed at me and abandoned me at my lowest. I thank all the men that took advantage of me, because every single person, every single experience helped me decide, change, and become the person I am now. I thank Rimgaile for encouraging me to write this book and for helping me become a better person. I thank my family for the support and all experiences. I thank God for helping me every day of my life.

**Never forget only you can change your life, now go enjoy it!**

# If Your Loved One Has an Addiction

## For the family members of the ones who have addiction

Thank you for sticking by the people you love. You must love them very much. Now the time has come that you probably waited for your whole relationship. They finally decided. But are you ready for it? Your life will change too. I am sorry to tell you that it will not be easy. It will be way harder than you think. Especially because if you don't understand the addiction, you don't know how hard it is. The person you love will change. There might be a lot of anger, guilt, shame, shyness, struggle, and change of moods at first. They might be more reserved, strict, moody, you might not even like that person anymore, because that is not the same person you fell in love with. If your choice is still to stick with them, remember this, no matter how hard the times will get, you can NEVER use these words: "You were nicer when you drank," "Just go and have a drink already," or "It is not my fault you are an alcoholic."

Trust me, you will have those moments. Do everyone a favor and just walk away. Do not open your mouth. Sometimes all it takes for them to go back are these words. You don't want to be the reason they returned to their addiction again. So, better walk away now, if you are not ready for the change and all that comes with it. Just leave. You might be able to come back later. It doesn't mean you are leaving forever, but if you don't think you are ready to be 100% supportive, just leave. They will be OK once they decide. They will be fine. They will go through the steps and get stronger. And honestly, they might not even like you anymore.

So, make a choice and stick to it, just like they must. Always be supportive, but also take care of yourself. I really hope you get to stick next to them and enjoy a new life with them.

# Acknowledgments

Thank you to my wonderful children, my mom, my brother, and Solveiga. I appreciate you supporting me regardless of the situation.

I'm grateful to my spiritual coach Rimgaile Aciene, who helped me find my purpose in life and strongly encouraged me to write this book.

I thank God and my angels for protecting me every single day and giving me all the amazing things that I have.

# About the Author

Greta Kudirkaite (writing under Greta Kay) is a multiple business owner, consultant, and mother of two beautiful children, devoted to helping people beat alcohol addiction and change their lives.

Let her help others! If you know someone who cannot afford a copy of the book, email GretaKay Books@gmail.com and share their story.

Greta has a course that can help you get rid of your addiction and stay sober. Reach out via email: GretaKayBooks@gmail.com.

NOTE: There is a Lithuanian version of this book available. Please purchase the English Kindle version and send your order receipt to GretaKayBooks@gmail.com. Greta will then send you the Lithuanian version.

www.ingramcontent.com/pod-product-compliance
Lightning Source LLC
Chambersburg PA
CBHW021121080526
44587CB00010B/599